T0197431

MIGUELITO
AND THE
MEAN BILLY GOAT

MIGUEL GARZA

AuthorHouse™
1663 Liberty Drive
Bloomington, IN 47403
www.authorhouse.com
Phone: 833-262-8899

Because of the dynamic nature of the Internet, any web addresses or links contained in this book may have changed since publication and may no longer be valid. The views expressed in this work are solely those of the author and do not necessarily reflect the views of the publisher, and the publisher hereby disclaims any responsibility for them.

Any people depicted in stock imagery provided by Getty Images are models, and such images are being used for illustrative purposes only.
Certain stock imagery © Getty Images.

This book is printed on acid-free paper.

ISBN: 978-1-6655-6948-4 (sc)
ISBN: 978-1-6655-6949-1 (e)

Print information available on the last page.

Library of Congress Control Number: 2022916087

Published by AuthorHouse 08/30/2022

authorHOUSE®

MIGUELITO
AND THE
MEAN BILLY GOAT

Once upon a time there was this little boy named Miguelito.

Miguelito lived on a farm

3

With Chickens, Cows, Horses, Rabbits,

Dogs, Cats and a
Big Mean Billy Goat.

One day Miguelito and his Brother were bored. "What do you want to do today?" asked Brother.

"I know!" said Miguelito. "Lets see who can run through the Goat corral without the Mean Billy Goat getting us."

"Ok!" said Brother.

Brother went first.

"Go, Brother!" said Miguelito.

"No, the Mean Billy Goat is too close,

let him get further away," said Brother.

The Mean Billy Goat walked away slowly looking back at Miguelito and Brother. The Mean Billy Goat knew what they wanted to do.

Brother jumped in and ran as fast as he could. The Mean Billy Goat did not like anyone in his Corral. The Mean Billy Goat put his head down and ran full speed at Brother.

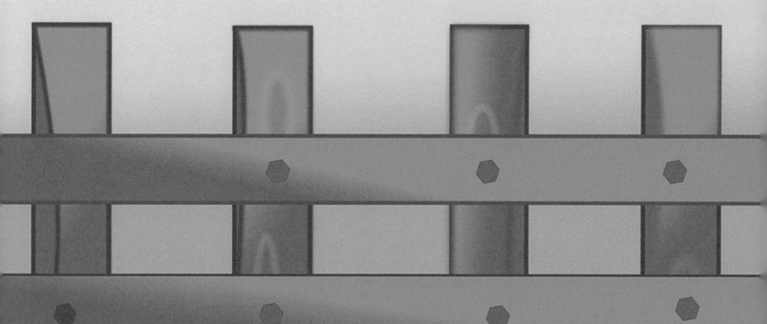

"Run, Run Brother!" Said
Miguelito. "Run! The Mean Billy Goat is coming after you."

Brother ran as fast as he could. Brother's eyes were wide with fear. He could feel the Mean Billy Goat catching up to him. As Brother got to the other side of the Corral, he grabbed the fence and climbed over just in time. The Mean Billy Goat tapped the fence with his head as Brother looked at him from outside the Corral.

Now it was Miguelito's turn.

"Now Miguelito!" said Brother.

"No, let the Mean Billy Goat get to the other side!"

Miguelito needed a little more time than Brother because Miguelito was kind of "Chubby." The Mean Billy Goat walked to the other side of the Corral.

Looking back at Miguelito he looked like he was smiling. Miguelito got on top of the fence and looked at The Mean Billy Goat. Miguelito jumped in and ran as fast as he could but of course Miguelito was kind of "Chubby." The Mean Billy Goat put his head down and ran full speed at Miguelito.

"Run, Run!" said Brother.

"Run, The Mean Billy Goat is coming after you!"

Miguelito ran as fast as he could. Dust was flying from Miguelito's feet, his eyes were wide open, his arms were swinging as fast as he could. Miguelito could feel the Mean Billy Goat catching up to him but remember Miguelito was kind of "Chubby."

Miguelito was getting closer to the fence and the Mean Billy Goat was getting closer to Miguelito. As Miguelito grabbed the fence to pull himself over the fence. The Mean Billy Goat raised his head and tapped Miguelito on the butt and threw him over the fence. Miguelito and Brother rolled on the ground laughing and laughing. The Mean Billy Goat seemed to be laughing also as he nodded his head up and down.

"That was fun," said Miguelito
"but let's not do that again!"

Printed in the United States
by Baker & Taylor Publisher Services